Ship Captain's Daughter

Ship Captain's Daughter

~

Growing Up on the Great Lakes

Ann M. Lewis

WISCONSIN HISTORICAL SOCIETY PRESS

Published by the Wisconsin Historical Society Press
Publishers since 1855
© 2015 by the State Historical Society of Wisconsin

wisconsinhistory.org

All photos are from the author's family collection unless otherwise noted.
The cover photo shows the author's daughter, Amy Michler Lewis (married
name Hunter), at age four, as she watches her grandfather's ship, the SS *Herbert C. Jackson,* enter the Duluth canal.

Printed in Canada
Cover design by Shawn Biner, Biner Design
Typesetting by Integrated Composition Systems, Spokane, Washington

19 18 17 16 15   1 2 3 4 5

Library of Congress Cataloging-in-Publication Data
Lewis, Ann M.
   Ship captain's daughter : growing up on the Great Lakes /
Ann M. Lewis. — 1st edition.
       pages cm
   ISBN 978-0-87020-730-3 (pbk. : alk. paper) —
ISBN 978-0-87020-731-0 (e-book)
   1. Lewis, Ann M.—Childhood and youth.   2. Ship captains—
Minnesota—Duluth—Biography.   3. Ship captains—Family relation-
ships—Anecdotes.   4. Seafaring life—Great Lakes (North America)—
Anecdotes.   5. Girls—Minnesota—Duluth—Biography.   6. Great
Lakes Region (North America)—Biography.   7. Duluth (Minn.)—
Social life and customs—20th century.   8. Duluth (Minn.)—Biography.
I. Title.   II. Title: Growing up on the Great Lakes.
   VK139.L49   2015
   386'.244092—dc23   [B]   2015018771

∞ The paper used in this publication meets the minimum requirements of
the American National Standard for Information Sciences—Permanence
of Paper for Printed Library Materials, ANSI Z39.48–1992.

To my parents Willis C. Michler and Dagmar A. Michler
my husband Herb
my children Amy and Lee
my son-in-law Jay and daughter-in-law Tiffany
my grandchildren Chloe, Sophie, and Herbie
and to all the people of the lake

Some went down to the sea in ships, doing business on the mighty waters.

—Psalm 107

Contents

My father, Captain Willis C. Michler, stands next to the pilothouse of the SS *Calumet*, his second command. The four stripes on his sleeve designate his status as ship's master.

Introduction

The ship comes in, the ship goes out. As the daughter of a Great Lakes ship captain, I grew up to the rhythm of the transport of iron ore. From the arrival of the shipping orders in March to "lay up" in December, from climbing the ship's ladder weekly to see my father while he was in port to watching his ship disappear again over the horizon line, my life was dominated by the excitement, the loneliness, the drama, and the lure of the shipping industry and the water.

My hometown of Duluth, Minnesota, is located at the western tip of Lake Superior. The water has always been the life of Duluth and its sister city, Superior, Wisconsin, where my father grew up. When iron ore was discovered in northern Minnesota and Wisconsin in the late 1800s, the Twin Ports, with their natural harbor, made it possible for giant cargo ships to carry ore from the mines in the north down through the Soo Locks to the steel mills on the lower lakes in the east. For generations, many local men have worked as shipbuilders, dockworkers, chandlers, uniform manufacturers, stevedores, and bridge tenders.

And then there are those men who have worked on the lake. My father, Willis Carl Michler, was one of them. He sailed the Great Lakes for forty-seven years and was a captain of thirteen different ships for twenty-one of those years. Drawn to the water and the big ships as a young man, he followed a dream of becoming a Great Lakes ship captain, and he and my mother and I lived it out together, in all its rich and varied and demanding dimensions.

My father's sailing career spanned the height of Great Lakes iron ore shipping, the lows of the Great Depression, World War II

My dad's ship rests at the dock in Ashland, Wisconsin, a seventy-mile drive from the Twin Ports of Duluth-Superior. The dock was built in 1915 to load ships with iron ore mined on the Gogebic Range of eastern Wisconsin and western Michigan.

(during which time the sailors served the country as members of the Merchant Marine), the opening of the St. Lawrence Seaway, the advent of radar, and the development of the taconite trade. He sailed before the invention of computers, GPS, cell phones, email, and Skype—and before sailors could apply for summer vacations. When I was growing up, we relied on letters Dad mailed from ports throughout the Great Lakes, calls from pay phones, and rare ship-to-shore calls. Today the ships that traverse the Great Lakes can be tracked on the internet. Many are twice the size of the freighters my dad first sailed, though at this writing, my father's last command, the SS *Herbert C. Jackson*, is still sailing, albeit with modern renovations. Instead of raw iron ore, the ships now carry taconite pellets and varied other cargoes such as coal and grain. Yet for those who continue to work on the ships, some things remain unchanged—the urgency to deliver cargo quickly, the challenges of weather, time away from family, and the power-ful call to a life on the water.

My father was the first in his family to have a career on the water. Historically, his people were people of the land. Settling in the Fond du Lac area of southern Wisconsin from the agricultural heartland of Germany, they were courageous, industrious, disci-plined, and religious. Some remained farmers, while others be-came blacksmiths. Two family members founded the Michler Company in Fond du Lac, crafting huge sleighs for use in Alaska and one for the Antarctic explorer Admiral Richard Byrd. One of them ran for mayor and helped found the family church. And one of them, my grandfather, left his people to become a conductor for the Soo Line Railroad Company in the northern Wisconsin port town of Superior, on the shores of the world's largest fresh-water lake.

At the age of sixteen, at the urging of *his* father and with the tools of his heritage plus his own romantic spirit, my father sailed out to sea. Ultimately, he became a Great Lakes ship captain.

From time to time, people have asked me what this life was like—what my father was like, what my mother's life was like, and what it was like to be the ship captain's daughter. The stories preserved in this book are my attempt to capture that lifestyle—the cycles of waiting and bursts of excitement, the vital connection to the lake itself—experienced by Great Lakes shipping families like my own.

The Shipping Season Begins

We were people of the lake. When Lake Superior started to thaw, we started to wait. Most people in Duluth welcomed spring. For our family, it was the beginning of the end, not only of winter, but also of our land time together. When the days grew longer and the ice on Lake Superior began to break up, Dad's shipping orders were soon to come. Every day they didn't was a relief. But sooner or later, inevitably, there they would be, jutting out of the mailbox in the long envelope marked The Interlake Steamship Company.

The house grew quiet, but the tempo of Dad's preparations for departure picked up. So much to do before leaving for the new sailing season: fix that leaky faucet at Grandma's, pick up the new glasses, go to the bank, finish up at the dentist, drain the gas out of the snowblower, and get the lawn mower ready for Mom. Finally, Dad went up to the attic and dragged down the big canvas duffel bag with his name stenciled on it, and the little black bag containing the tools of his trade—star chart, quadrant, compass, slide rule. Then he started packing again.

Anticipation grew daily. Calls started coming in from the other sailors in the fleet: "What cook did you get?" "Who is your chief engineer?" Most importantly, "Who is your captain, and what's the name of your ship? Same as last year, or did you 'move up'?" (Salaries were related to the size of the ship.)

In late March, my dad's ship follows the ice cutter's path from the ports of Duluth and Superior out to the open lake.

No more help for me with math homework. No more listening to Dad play the piano into the night. Mother always wanted to have friends over for dinner one last time, but there was no more time. All of that was over. From now until the lake froze over again, we were back on "sailing time." From March until December, we would live our family life in the spaces that we could find in between the loading, unloading, and shipping of ore.

Some ships laid up for the winter across the bay in Superior at Fraser Shipyards. Dad's ships, however, always laid up in the lower lakes "down below" the Soo Locks at dry docks in Chicago, Ashtabula, Cleveland, or Toledo. In later years, the sailors flew to and from their ships to begin and end the season. When I was young, however, Dad always took the train. Even when life became more informal, he always wore his best suit, tie, and hat to mark this important occasion.

Dad prepares to leave for the old Milwaukee Road depot from my aunt's house in St. Paul, Minnesota, after a going-away dinner.

Once his ship was fitted out and had set sail, the familiar ritual of calculating his weekly arrival to our area began. The *Duluth News Tribune* posted the times that the ships passed through the Soo Locks. About twenty-six hours after locking up, he would arrive in the Twin Ports. If he went through the locks at six on a Tuesday morning, he would be due in at about eight on Wednesday morning, which meant Mom would miss her ten a.m. church circle that week. If he left at one on Wednesday afternoon to go back down, he would be at the Soo at three p.m. on Thursday, in port at ten p.m. on Friday, unloaded by eight a.m. on Saturday, back up bound through the Soo by four p.m. on Sunday, and at a dock near us again at six a.m. on Monday. Now the school conference for Monday at nine a.m. might have to be canceled, but then again, there just might be a chance that Dad could get off the ship to come with us and meet the teacher, if the weather didn't delay him, or if someone didn't decide to quit and have to be officially terminated and paid off. On the day of my eighth-grade graduation, I remember we got lucky. Dad got in at seven a.m. and was able to get off right away. He had to be back by noon, but he got to see my new dress, hear my piano piece, and help Mom and me pick lilacs in the backyard for the punch table.

When he came to the Twin Ports, he entered the harbor through either the Duluth or Superior entry. The Duluth entry was the best, with its grand and picturesque Aerial Bridge. Especially when I was a child, I used to love to go down to the pier and watch his ship come in. Ideally, we would be there much earlier—in time to watch him break the horizon line. For a long time the boat seemed to barely move. After about a half hour, however, it began growing in size, approaching slowly but steadily, and finally, it came in fast.

"Get ready," Mom would say. "Here he comes." The tourists at the pier started running—some out to the lighthouse to watch the great ship enter the canal—while others sat right on the breakwater. Our favorite place was on the walkway by the marine museum. We watched proudly as the huge ship glided down the canal to tower above us. "Look up," Mom would say, and there would be Dad. He'd lift up the big black bullhorn with both hands and in a booming voice yell out, "Ahoy, mates! Forty minutes to the dock." And I'd yell back, "Ahoy, Papa!"

Whether in Duluth or Superior, the docks were all alike. We parked our car by the gatehouse, showed our passes to the guard, and picked our way along the rocky dirt road leading to the stairway that went down to the water. The docks were built to load on both sides, so there was a walkway through the middle. Ore trains rolling out to the ships rumbled on the tracks overhead. Their

Dad's ship, locking up from the lower lakes to the level of Lake Superior, at the Soo Locks, through which all ships traversing the lakes must pass

brakes screeched when they stopped, scaring the pigeons from their perches on the rafters above us. Even though shafts of light broke in from the outside, it was still dark in there, like in a dimly lit tunnel.

On either side of the walkway, there were surge holes. Dirty water slurped over the edges, splashing over our shoes and getting the cement wet. Way down at the end, we sometimes spotted a sailor who had just gotten off his ship to come ashore. It was like looking through the wrong end of the binoculars. The tiny figure got closer and closer, and bigger and bigger, until one of us had to step aside to let the other pass. Sometimes we could smell his aftershave!

Even if it wasn't raining, something always dripped, and there were always loud noises: spouts grinding up and down, whistles, and people yelling orders. If the ore had gotten wet in the open

The eighty-foot-high Ashland, Wisconsin, dock with train cars and dockworkers visible on the top. It was torn down beginning in 2012.

train cars, it wouldn't run into the hold. On the catwalks, men
rhythmically pounded the chutes with long steel rods to break
the ore loose. *Kaboom-oom-oom.* The sound echoed in waves off
the steel girders.

When I got scared, Mom took my hand and we began to
march and sing: "Be kind to your fine feathered friends, da da da
da da da da da ..." Then, through the spaces between the columns,
we began to see the ship: first the steering pole, then the forward
anchor, then the pilothouse, then the winches, the hatches, and
the ladder. Finally we heard my dad yelling, "Hey! Here come
my girls!"

To get aboard ship to see Dad, we had to climb the ladder.
When I was young, my dad carried me up. He held me in the
curve of his left arm, and with his right hand he grabbed and let
go, grabbed and let go, lurching from rung to rung as we went up.
At the top, he turned and let go of the ladder, jumping onto the

The ladder we used for boarding the SS *Calumet* is in position for storage, with another ship visible in the background waiting to unload with Huletts (machine-operated buckets).

landing and then down onto the deck. When I was older, I climbed the ladder by myself, pretending I was brave. My father bragged about it, but he always stood nervously at the iron platform that hung over the side of the ship reaching out to "catch me" at the top. When I gave him my left hand, he pulled it toward him, quickly taking my right hand as I stepped onto the iron grate.

Sometimes I still dream about it.

If there was a wind, the cables would whine and stretch, letting the ship drift out a little, leaving a foot or two of open water between the ship and the dock. When I looked down to put my foot on the landing, I could see the open space. The ore drippings

The Duluth, Missabe, and Iron Range (DMIR) dock, built in 1918, was the dock closest to our home. Ore for this dock was transported by train from the Iron Range's open pit mines sixty miles to the north.

made the water rusty brown. If I fell, there would be no way to save me. I was always relieved to make it up, but during the whole time I was aboard I worried about getting back down.

For most of my early childhood, Dad was a first mate. Because the mate is in charge of loading the ship, it's hard for him to get off for more than an hour or two to come home for a visit. During those early years Mother and I spent a lot of time aboard ship visiting him. I stood with him out on deck. I watched as he cupped his hands around his mouth and shouted up at the dock boss on the train track high above us. He'd yell, "It's a two-car pocket," or maybe he'd say three. I didn't know what that meant, but it sounded important. It was all very important, Dad said, because if he didn't get the cargo loaded evenly, the ship would roll. When he was loading, I couldn't really talk to him. I just stood beside him.

The big black spouts poured the ore from the train cars into the ship. Wide at the top and narrow at the bottom, they roared like angry lions as they dropped down from the dock into the hatches. When Dad gave the signal to open the chute, a few rocks bounced down, then a few clumps came, and then big rushes of rust-colored dirt flowed into the hatch. I'd take Dad's hand and lean over, looking down into the hold, watching as the pile grew higher and higher, thinking of what it would be like to fall in there. The loading started from the back and then skipped up to the front. The middle was loaded last to keep everything balanced. When all the hatches were half full, suddenly everything stopped. The whole operation came to a standstill, and the dockworkers took a break while the rest of the ballast (the water in the tanks that kept the empty ship steady) was pumped out. Before loading could be completed, all the ballast water had to be out of the tanks. That took about an hour. Now Dad could leave the deck.

Before going up to Dad's quarters, we always went into the mess hall for donuts and coffee, or leftover desserts, or sometimes

The off-watch crew waits to go ashore.

my favorite—bologna and mustard sandwiches on toasted white bread. I loved the mess hall. There was always a lot of food to choose from, because the cook kept out what was called "night lunch"—even if it was eaten in the daytime—for the men who missed meals due to their work schedules. The galley was warm and smelled like melted butter. Dockworkers and sailors stood around talking or sat on the stools at the long crew's table with their work gloves stuffed into their back pockets.

After our snack, we walked up forward to Dad's quarters. Mom was already there, knitting or reading. She'd put in her years on deck, so usually, after saying hello to everyone, she went up to Dad's room to wait for the break. Sometimes she took her sketch pad and drew pictures of the ships or the harbor. Sometimes she did Dad's laundry.

Dad's room had only two chairs. I sat on the bed, which was on a metal platform. Mother showed him the mail, had him sign some things, or talked about what was on the cover of the *Time*

Mom knits in the captain's quarters on the SS *Charles M. Schwab*. Her knitting instructions are on the pillow.

magazine she'd brought him. Maybe she gave him some photographs, or letters, or an article from the paper.

While they talked, I pulled the heavy maroon bed curtains around me and pretended I was a movie star, or I fell asleep. After a while there was a loud whistle from the dock, Mother picked up her book or knitting, and Dad and I went back out on deck to finish the load and do the "trim"—the final distribution of cargo.

Adventures in Port

Most visits were pretty much the same, but there is one I will never forget, thanks to the bumboat. Dad and I were out on deck. He was writing down figures in his black leather loading book, and I was passing the time by counting how many spouts there were in a ship's length, and then how many pigeons I could see.

Then (hooray!) I saw the bumboat scooting around the corner, bouncing over the water. It was like watching a cartoon character pull alongside. The little floating store was black with a yellow wheelhouse and a hemp bumper on the bow that looked like a mustache. Most intriguing was the mysterious door through which everyone disappeared.

Why was everyone so eager to go down there? I stood beside Dad watching as the men started to line up, slinging their legs over the railing, and scrambling straight down. Would I ever dare to do that? "No," I said to myself, "I would not!" Just looking at the boat surging up and down on the waves made me dizzy. I watched with interest, however, as the men climbed back up with bags full of candy, magazines, clothes, cigarettes, and even an occasional transistor radio. Suddenly, I saw Mr. Kaner, the owner and captain, pop out the door. He had a mustache that looked just like the bumper on the bow of the boat, reminding me of Groucho Marx. Looking up, he waved, pointed to the door, and yelled, "Hi, Bill. Come on down."

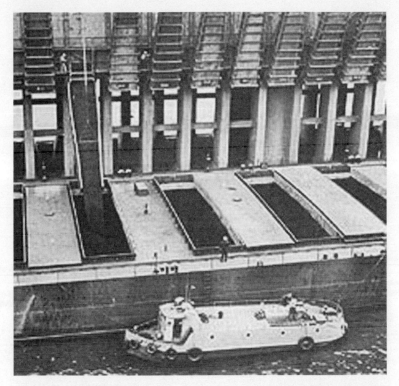

A bumboat at the Great Northern docks in Allouez outside of Superior, Wisconsin. The bumboats were floating convenience stores owned by the Kaner brothers of Superior. They are no longer in service due to the decrease in the number of ships on the Great Lakes and the ability to order from the internet.

I couldn't believe it when Dad turned to me and said, "Do you want to go?"

I gulped. "Well, um, maybe, kind of . . ." I looked warily at the ladder. "You can do it," Dad said. "I'll be right below you." He slung his leg over the railing. Then he told me to turn around and bend backward under the wire as he guided my right foot down to the first rung. Then he drew down my left foot. Now my toes were resting right against the steel ship. There was no angle to this ladder, just straight up and down. It wiggled as I took my next step. I froze and sucked in my breath. Dad kept one hand on my leg.

"It's okay," he said. "Keep going."

I started again. When I felt my first foot on the deck, I started to breathe again. He took my hand, and we made our way to the little door. Four steps down and, pyew! The smell of sweet tobacco made me gag. I plugged my nose and hesitated, but the cheery calendar girls smiling and winking all around were very welcoming, not to mention the ladies on the covers of magazines on the book rack. Half of our ship's crew was in there, talking and laughing, drinking beer and smoking and telling jokes. No other girls in there, that's for sure!

Dad quickly steered me around to the back, which was so crowded that I disappeared in between the cases of watches, bins of underwear and socks, boxes of birthday cards, bottles of perfume, razors, aftershave, and columns of cartons of Camels and Lucky Strikes. All sizes of transistor radios covered the walls from floor to ceiling. I noticed a whole section of cough medicines and a display of Brylcreem with a big cardboard picture of a man with curly dark brown hair and a blond woman with her hand behind his ear. What I liked best of all, though, were the boxes of candy and gum lined up in double rows in front of the cash register right next to the cigarette lighters.

Behind the register stood Mr. Kaner, who was gruff, gravelly voiced, and kind of scary to a young customer like myself. He seemed to know everyone by name and was passing on the news from the last ship, where he had just seen a sailor who had previously been on our ship. When he saw me, his bushy eyebrows shot up in surprise. I took a step backward, but he came around the counter, bent down, and made a big fuss over me, telling me that I was beautiful and that I had been brave to come down. Afterward, he took me over to the freezer and let me pick out a free ice cream bar. Dad bought a Dreamsicle for himself, and we said good-bye to Mr. Kaner and went out on deck to eat our treats.

Standing in the stern of Dad's ship at the Great Northern ore docks in Superior, Wisconsin, Mom wonders where Dad and I have gone.

When we'd finished, we stuck our sticks in the big ash can with all the cigarette butts and went over to the ladder. We looked up and—uh-oh—saw Mom glaring down at us. "I think we're in trouble," Dad said.

It was a little easier going up. I didn't stop once, and I tried not to look scared, but after Dad helped push me under the wire again and then got himself back on deck, I heard my mother whisper to him, "Willis Carl Michler, what were you thinking! Don't you ever take that girl down there again!" Dad and I winked at each other.

I don't think the ladder was her main concern.

When the load was done, Mom and I hugged Dad good-bye and climbed down the ship's ladder, which was a little lower now with all the ore in the hold. The deckhands let go of the cables; the ship started backing out of the slip, and Dad sailed off for another five-and-a-half-day trip.

In the fall, my teacher taught a unit on Duluth, the harbor, and the sailing life. She told the class that my dad was a sailor. She asked me if it was exciting to have a dad who worked on an ore freighter.

"It is when the bumboat comes," I answered. I don't think she knew what I meant.

This life had many memorable moments, but they were totally unpredictable. For example, Dad occasionally carried a load of coal to Washburn, Wisconsin, seventy miles down the Wisconsin shore. Unloading coal took a long time, and didn't require much oversight by the first mate. Here, in a town with only one dock on a sandy beach, that could mean a walk in the lakefront park, a visit by ferry to Madeline Island, or, in the fall, a drive inland to visit an apple orchard. On one such layover my dad even triumphantly climbed the fire tower up on the hill of the neighboring town of Bayfield, as he'd once done as a teenage boy. These deviations from the routine were full of a sense of stolen time, of sheer luck. When such moments came along, we dropped everything and grabbed them.

One such window of opportunity came the summer I was eight. Dad was delivering cargo "down below" in Sandusky, Ohio, when the steelworkers went out on strike. Dad was marooned, his ship tied up for an indefinite amount of time. The strike could end at any time, but it seemed that the sides were deadlocked, and the ships wouldn't set sail again until matters were resolved. The question was, would the striking workers hold out long enough for Mom and me to drive all the way to Ohio? And if so, could Mom do it? She would either have to drive from Duluth to Chicago and then all the way around the bottom of Lake Michigan, or go through Wisconsin to Manitowoc, take the ferry across Lake Michigan to Ludington, Michigan, and then continue south to Sandusky.

A flurry of phone calls went back and forth. Mom looked at

the map one more time and then she decided, "We can do it!" The next morning we were off. She chose to go to Manitowoc. We packed our clothes, put sandwiches and coffee in our Scotch cooler, and started out. Sandusky, here we come!

We drove for hours, arriving at the ferry dock after dark. Men directed our car into the wide mouth of the car carrier, after which we climbed out and walked between the cars to the stairway up to the lounge. We found a bench to sit on, and I finally fell asleep. It was the middle of the night by the time we got off—too late to get our money's worth from staying in a motel, Mom said—so we slept in the car for a few hours in the ferry parking lot. We started off again at first light, listening to Arthur Godfrey on the radio as we drove along. By midmorning, with only a few hours of sleep, Mom was starting to look really tired.

It was after lunch that we finally passed the "Welcome to Sandusky" sign, but we still had to find the shipyards. After stopping at a gas station to ask directions and making a few wrong turns, finally the guardhouse came into view. We pulled up and were just getting out to ask if we could call Dad on the phone, when the door of the little house opened and out he popped, in shorts instead of his usual work clothes. The trip turned out to be well worth it, as we stayed in Sandusky for two weeks.

Dad was still a first mate then and had only one room for quarters, but the captain let us stay in the guest rooms on board and even use the lounge, which had a little TV in a big blond wood cabinet. My mother thought that was very "modern."

As the first mate, Dad was in charge of the crew, but there wasn't much to do while they waited for the strike to end except scrape and paint the deck and do other maintenance jobs. The men still served their watches but could leave the ship when they were off duty. Sometimes a group would walk together up to the little collection of gas stations and convenience stores out

My parents and I onboard the ship in Sandusky as we wait for the strike to end

on the road. Other times the men would talk and play cards with the crews of the other ships with which we were tied up. Dad's ship was one of four ships in a group, and we had to walk across the planks connecting them to go ashore. The good thing was that the pier where we were tied up was equipped with a stationary ramp to get on and off, rather than a ladder.

It was hot, and the crew was out on deck most of the time. We had an air conditioner in one porthole, but it was very noisy, so we were usually on deck, too. Dad got the men to tell stories. Oscar had been in the war and talked about the rain and mud in the trenches. He had a Norwegian accent and liked to shave outside. He had been a shoemaker in the war and fixed everyone's shoes now, including his own, by flipping the soles over when they began to wear out. Tony could draw cartoons, though mostly he drew figures of curvy women with short skirts, high boots, and long hair. Harry was from Tennessee and played the fiddle. He talked to my mother about his own mother. He was homesick.

During the strike in Sandusky, I take a turn sweeping on deck, while a couple of the deckhands, Tony and Harry, look on.

One day, for something to do, the men threw a firecracker at a seagull. The bird swooped after it and squawked hysterically when it blew up. They all laughed. I thought it was mean but I laughed too so that I wouldn't look like a sissy.

Most importantly, we had a car and could go off on excursions. That meant we could go to Catawba Island, which was magical. It had an amusement park that glittered at night and a beautiful beach where I learned how to swim. One afternoon, we were sitting on the beach on our blanket after eating our ship provisions of pork sandwiches and cupcakes, and suddenly Dad said, "Everyone in the water." I loved the water, but I didn't know how to swim. We ran in hand in hand, Mom on one side and Dad on the other, and kept running until I couldn't touch bottom anymore. They held me up as I began to float and then suddenly, Dad put his arm under my stomach and flipped my legs up parallel to the water and let me go.

"Paddle," he shouted, and he moved his hands up and down dog-paddle style. I did, wildly, but my legs kept sinking down and down, and the water was coming up over my chin. As I was screaming and flailing, Dad rescued me, pulling my legs back up parallel to the water. Then he pushed me off again, yelling, "Kick *and* paddle." I started paddling like mad, kicking at the same time, and suddenly I was swimming. We swam together all afternoon and then dried off in the late-afternoon sun.

Dad's First Command

The following year, 1953, started out the same. Dad left in mid-March when the lake thawed, and Mother started checking the paper again for his estimated weekly arrival times at ports near us. April went by, and May and June, and then, that July, it happened—I was no longer the daughter of a first mate. Our whole world changed. Just before my ninth birthday, my dad became a captain.

The significance of this event is difficult to convey. Promotions were awarded strictly by seniority and the availability of ships. Ore contracts dictated how many ships were in service. The men on the officer's track took their various licenses—weather plotting, navigational aids, piloting—and then they waited. The line of succession was long.

When my father first realized his dream of "getting a ship to sail," thirty-six ships made up the Interlake Steamship fleet. As of this writing, there are nine.

It happened like this. Dad was returning to Duluth with a ship, and Mom learned that he was due to arrive at the Duluth, Mesabi, and Iron Range dock in Duluth at two a.m. She wouldn't let me go with her to meet the ship in the middle of the night, so my grandparents came and stayed over.

Late that night I heard Mom's alarm clock ring. Then I heard her lock the back door and start the car. I fell back asleep. The

The SS *Adriatic* was Dad's first command and the ship my family remembered with enduring fondness. JIM DAN HILL MARINE ARCHIVES, UNIVERSITY OF WISCONSIN–SUPERIOR

next thing I heard was the refrigerator door open and close, and voices in the kitchen, and I realized Dad was able to get off the ship for a visit. They were home!

I got up and crept down the stairs, wanting to surprise them. But just when I came around the corner, I saw Dad pulling the cork out of a bottle of wine, and the two of them burst out laughing. I didn't know what to do, so I just stopped and listened.

"I couldn't believe it," Dad said. "I heard that they might, and then I heard that they weren't going to, and then the skipper told me the news." He sat down and started eating a cold leftover pork chop, and Mom toasted him with her glass.

I'd better go upstairs, I thought. But just as I was turning around, Dad looked up and saw me. "I thought I heard something over there. Come here, sleepyhead, and join the party."

As I walked toward him, he jumped up to give me a hug, and then he surprised me by pushing me back at arm's length. Putting his hands on my shoulders, he looked at me as if he meant business.

"Guess what, doll? They're pulling out another ship. They're moving more ore this summer than they have since the war, and they're fitting her out right now in Buffalo! And you know what?" He grinned. "Your dad is going to be the captain. After twenty-seven years on the deck, your dad is going to be The Old Man!'"

"Wow!" I said, as enthusiastically as I could.

Of course, I knew this was a big thing. I had heard the story about how, years before, Dad had narrowly escaped a loss in seniority when my grandmother was severely ill. He had asked for a leave, which was not granted. At that time it was unheard of even to ask. He did get off for a couple of weeks, and upon his return there was no job available. After pleading his case at the home office, he eventually got rehired. The five years of service he had accrued were saved. It was wartime, and it was finally decided that while he had been away, he was officially in the Merchant Marine. The service time was credited, and as a result my dad had the seniority required to be promoted without having to wait for the next opportunity.

I knew that, but Mom wanted to make sure I realized how important this was. She reached over and pulled me onto her lap, looked me in the eye, and said, "Do you really know what this means? It means that your dad will be up on his own deck, that he will have a bedroom, an office, and an observation room [a room the length of the front cabin ringed with portholes], and even a couch. It means he can get off when he is in port without asking and without trading watches. It means he will go to the meetings with the captains and chiefs. It means he will make more money. It means everything, that's what it means. It means we've been waiting for this our whole lives!"

"And," Dad said to Mom, "it means that you now have thirty

Dad standing proudly on the "captain's deck"

sailing days. And guess what?" he said to me. "When you turn twelve, you can take trips, too."

"It means," he said, raising his glass to Mom, "that you are the wife of a ship captain! And that you," he said, turning to me, "are the ship captain's daughter!"

Dad's first ship, the *Adriatic*, was half the length of the current fleet's flagship. It was coal-fired and old, but the captain's quarters

The captain's quarters of the SS *Adriatic* with its beautiful bookcase, and above it, the big brass ship's clock that chimed every half hour, day and night.

were constructed of beautiful wood. To our family, it was the *Queen Mary.*

Many things did change after that night. But some things in the sailing life never do. It was true, Dad didn't have to load the ship anymore, which meant, if there was no pressing business, it was possible for him to be the first man off and the last one on in port. But even as a captain, there were the basic facts of the sailing life, and the main one was, there was no getting away from "sailing time."

Now, Dad arranged for the dock boss to call when the ship was an hour or so away from being loaded. That was technically enough advance notice to make it back to the ship on time. But we lived in Duluth, and if the ship was docked at the Great Northern Ore docks across the bay in Superior, he'd have to cross the bridge. That was the "wild card," as my mother said. The old Interstate Bridge opened for any passing ship.

Interstate Bridge, Duluth, Minn.

The Old Interstate Bridge spanned the bay between Duluth and Superior. When it swung open for passing ships, it stopped traffic for an average of twenty minutes. It was replaced by the High Bridge in 1961, but a remnant of the old bridge remains as a fishing platform. ARCHIVES AND SPECIAL COLLECTIONS, KATHRYN A. MARTIN LIBRARY, UNIVERSITY OF MINNESOTA–DULUTH

One night at the end of September, we got caught. Dad was home, and the dock boss called. We were just going out the door when Dad decided he'd better take his heavy wool mackinaw, as the weather could turn at any time now. He searched the front and back hall closets but couldn't find it. He went up to the attic to check the garment bags, but it wasn't there, either. Finally, it dawned on him; he had put it in the basement clothes locker under the stairs, the one with the mothballs in it. He ran down and grabbed it, shot outside, and headed for the car. But when he bent down to say good-bye to the dog, he noticed a screw missing in the gate latch and ran back in, got a screwdriver, and fixed it. By that time, we were running late.

Racing down Piedmont Avenue, we spotted trouble—a ship in the bay, headed for the bridge. It seemed like we could beat it, but by the time we got to Garfield Avenue, it wasn't looking good. Dad started gunning for the bridge, but just as we were about to go over, the warning bells went off—*ding, ding, ding*—and the big white arm came down. There we were, the first car behind the last car that made it.

Dad didn't swear in front of me very often, but this was one of the times that he did. Every minute's delay cost the company money, and the company was not forgiving. Watching the lights of the oncoming ship creeping toward the open span, the three of us sat in silence. In the glow of the lights of the dashboard, I could see my dad's cheek muscles clench and unclench. Mom even stopped talking.

After a few minutes, I looked out the back window and— wow!—the whole sky was full of magical shifting shafts of light over the hills of Duluth—green, white, and pale yellow columns, bleeding and blending into each other, as when you turn a kaleidoscope.

"Hey, look," I said, glad to break the silence.

"Holy Toledo!" Dad said. "I haven't seen an aurora borealis like that in ages."

I asked him what caused it, and he started to tell me about gases, and sunspots, and solar winds, and electrical charges, the arctic sun, and the earth's magnetic field, and how sometimes he would see this from out on the water along the North Shore. He made me say "aurora borealis" over and over again, and then we all started saying it, and then the bells started ringing. The big arm in front of us lifted, and the bridge locked back into place. Dad put the car in gear, and we were off, leading the parade of cars making low whining noises on the metal span. As soon as we got to the Superior side, Dad turned left onto a side street to avoid the traffic lights and floored it. Mom's knees hit the glove compartment when he jammed on the brakes. He thought he'd spotted a police car up ahead, but it was just a taxi.

When we passed Barker's Island going about a hundred miles an hour, we could see the beginning of the dock—but no ship. "Uh-oh," Dad said. "They must have shifted her back." In another five minutes, we were at the turn in Allouez, in South Superior. When we roared up to the guardhouse, we could see that there were no spouts down. The ore train was moving toward us and the ship was at the end of the dock, loaded. We screeched to a stop. Dad jumped out of the car, flashed his pass at the guard, and started running, without looking back or even saying good-bye.

"Goodbye, Willie," Mom muttered to herself.

We sat there for a minute, watching him. Then Mom slid over to the driver's seat, put the car in reverse, and turned around to back up. "Oh no!" she cried out. "He forgot his mackinaw!" She grabbed the coat and turned around, but he was gone. She slumped down in her seat. From the backseat, I could see a little tear run slowly down her cheek and land on her lip. She licked it, sucked in her breath, and then I watched as she rolled down the window and yelled at the top of her lungs, "I hate that bridge! And I hate steam boating!" The two of us drove home slowly.

That night it sounded like there was someone or something in the house—like an animal rustling around. I crept into my parents' bedroom, but Mom wasn't there, and then I heard the hangers banging around in the bedroom closet. I was about to investigate, when a voice from the back of the closet called out, "Willie? Willie, is that you?" (Mom was the only one who called Dad Willie.) Just then the telephone rang, and Mom stumbled past me into the hall, reaching for the phone.

Uh-oh, I thought. Sleepwalking again. Sometimes she did that before Dad called. She seemed to have a sixth sense about when he would be in port. Tonight, however, he would still be in the middle of Lake Superior, which meant it would be a ship-to-shore call, which also meant it must be important.

"Yes, yes. I'll accept the charges," she said.

They talked for quite a while, and then I heard her say, "Not even time for a good-bye?" I didn't understand it when she said, "Ours is a winter affair," but I giggled right out loud when, after a long silence, I heard her say, "Good-bye, sweet prince." I thought she was awake, but she must have still been dreaming.

A few days later, a local reporter called Mom, saying she wanted to do a feature article for the *Duluth News Tribune* about the ship captains' wives. It wasn't good timing. Mother had a feeling that the reporter already knew what she wanted to write. People loved to romanticize this life, and Mother wasn't in the mood. But the reporter was a woman and said she was eager to tell it like it really was, so Mom met with her and did just that.

"At home alone, a skipper's wife, of necessity, becomes a jack-of-all-trades," my mother told the reporter. "She not only has to learn to balance the checkbook, she becomes self-sufficient. She must learn to change a faucet's washer, do electrical repair work, clean the garage, and mow the lawn. A wife may accompany her captain husband on the lakes for up to a month of the season, but most of us break up the time—it would be too confining to stay aboard ship for a month at a time."

She went on to say that sometimes she was afraid of the weather. "Years ago a ship would head for the nearest port in a storm. Now, with modern technological advances, like radar to look ahead at the weather, the ship just keeps going. Those Lake Superior storms can be frightening.

"There could be a real morale booster," Mom continued. "If only a captain could have a week or two at home during the summer to see Duluth without overshoes and storm coats in its summer finery—without having to watch the clock for sailing time."

But then . . . "Night or day, it's always a thrill to go through the Soo Locks," she conceded, adding that Burns Harbor was her favorite port. "It's such a clean, lovely place compared to most other stops."

Sure enough, when the article appeared in the paper, the

The portrait of my parents that ran with the article in the *Duluth News Tribune*

Despite Its Periods of Separation

Life of Skipper's Wife Rewarding

BY JANET BURNS
Of The News-Tribune Staff

Duluth-Superior is not only the most beautiful port on the Great Lakes but the only place in which to live if you're married to a Great Lakes ship's captain.

So say Mrs. Willis Michler and Mrs. Harold Van Orman, both of whose spouses are skippers of ships of the Pickands Mather fleet. Capt. Michler runs the Herbert C. Jackson, one of the company's larger vessels. Capt. Van Orman is responsible for the Walter A. Watson. Michler has had his title for 18 years; Van Orman is in his second season as a captain.

It would be very frustrating to have a Duluth address, both wives say, if you were wed to a first mate. That officer is in charge of loading the raw ore or pellets. — he

Marys River, about 20 miles below the locks. Sailors refer to it as Sailor's Encampment since it was once the point at which sailing vessels tied up at night to await making the run through the locks in daylight hours.

"It's beautifully wooded," Mrs. Michler recalls, "with heavy underbrush. It's where children always stand along the banks shouting 'Captain, won't you blow us a salute?' — and he always does. It's a must to watch when we sail by, either by day or night."

"The rivers," Mrs. Van Orman continues, "are by far the most beautiful part of a trip, especially down the Detroit River by day. But I shall never forget the ugliness of the city during the summer riots a few years ago. The fires blazed fiercely against the night sky, smoke

A wife seldom leaves the ship in port. The main reason isn't hard to guess; three times out of four it's between one and six in the morning.

One duty of a captain's wife when aboard is to serve as hostess for guests who may be aboard. Sometimes she may become weary, but the VIPs are usually exciting to meet, both women said.

Guests — landlubbers all — have a favorite question, "Does your husband get home for weekends?" It seems to be an irritating question to a captain's wife who knows that a boat does not stop running at 5 p.m. Friday

Mrs. Michler has an unusual method of passing time aboard ship — she often takes along furniture that needs refurnishing. Mrs. Van Orman plans ahead and creates Christ-

boxes is a must. Most skippers do keep a garden away from home and give tender loving care to petunias and begonias — even to the extent of covering them in time of storm. Rain water is carefully saved for watering; each bloom is counted every day and the dying blossoms snipped to encourage new growth.

One unlucky captain not too many seasons ago dug into his window box to be bitten by a bat. The unfortunate man had to be rowed ashore to undergo rabies shots.

Mrs. Michler notes she sometimes is afraid of the weather. Years ago a ship would head for the nearest port in a storm. Now, with modern technological advances, like radar to look ahead at the weather, the ship just keeps going. Those

The newspaper article in which Mother shared her thoughts about her life as the wife of a ship captain appeared in the *Duluth News Tribune*. DULUTH NEWS TRIBUNE reporter had summed up the interview with the headline, "Life of Skipper's Wife Rewarding."

"Oh, no," I thought; she'll say, "I told you so." But included in the article was a picture of Mom and Dad in the pilothouse behind the wheel. They were smiling. I guess the picture must have brought back the good times, too, because she cut it out and put in on the refrigerator, where it stayed until it yellowed and faded. And surprisingly, she didn't say anything about the choice of title.

I Set Sail

Finally the summer of my twelfth birthday arrived, and I was old enough for my first sailing trip. It was exciting at first, especially the fire drill, when all the horns and whistles were blowing, but it wasn't long until the days dragged on a bit. The wind, water, and sky seemed endless. Lake Superior was the best for Dad, as after he cleared the breakwater, barring bad weather, it was twenty-six hours of open lake to the Soo Locks. There were always paperwork and occasional personnel issues, but for the most part, it was the time when he had a little break, to sleep, and read, and listen to classical music, which was his passion. Dad loved having us on board with him and tried to make it interesting and fun, but he was also used to solitude. He was able to sit for long periods of time thinking, working on projects, and not talking. For a passenger like me, some days could be long, especially when it was my birthday and nobody seemed to notice!

The day I turned twelve, Mom appeared to be asleep in the bedroom. Dad was sitting at his desk mending a transistor box, and I was just standing there watching. Then, suddenly, the telephone above his desk rang and the red light started blinking. It was the chief engineer inviting us back to the engine room.

"OK, Harvey," Dad said. "We'll be right back."

Whoopee! I thought. Something to do! We got on our jackets and quietly slipped out the door. I held Dad's arm as we walked

The engine room with all its gauges on the floating museum the SS *Irwin* moored in the Duluth harbor

back aft. Walking aft made me kind of dizzy, because the ship is moving forward while you're walking backward, so you're going backward and forward at the same time.

When we got to the middle of the after-cabin, Dad pushed down the handle of the heavy steel door. We stepped over the high coaming and turned around to go backward down the steep steps. It was like entering the inner workings of an enormous watch. Everything was ticking and whirring. The big pistons were going up and down, lights were blinking, the little wheels in the gauges were spinning, and in the middle was the chief engineer, sitting at his desk, drinking from his coffee mug. With no windows, the engine room was warm and smelled of oil.

"Well, hello there, young lady," the chief said. "You know, I had an idea." He took us to his tool bench and showed us a pile of blocks of wood that he'd cut out. "I thought we could make some little boats," he said. He took one piece of wood and nailed it on top of another larger piece, and then he nailed another little piece on top of that, and it did look like a boat. Then he screwed an eye hook in its bow that he had sawed into a point, tied some twine to it, and superglued a toothpick with a little American flag on top.

My dad laughed and said, "Blow me down, Harvey."

Then the chief looked at me and said, "Now you do it."

I picked up the hammer and the nails that he'd laid out, took the other big block of wood and nailed a little smaller one on top of it, and a little smaller one on top of that, and he screwed an eye hook in the front of it and put the flag on top. He put a long piece of twine through the eye hook, and then we went over to the gangway. He pushed down with all his might on the big clamps and opened the top half of the gangway door, which opened onto the deep blue Lake Superior water. The ship was loaded so the water was just a couple of feet below us.

He tied the twine around my wrist and threw the boat in. It bounced around a bit before diving under the water. He reached for the string and pulled it in, letting it back out slowly, and when he handed the string to me again the boat was floating. Then he gave the first one that he'd made to Dad, who threw it in. It bounced around a bit, and then it floated, too. We laughed and sailed our boats in the sun.

Then the chief turned to me and said, "I hear we have a birthday girl with us today." Dad winked, and I blushed. When we got back to our cabin, Mom had a birthday cake waiting with twelve candles. She and Mr. Gregory, the cook, had made it. I blew out the candles and made a wish for smooth seas and a daylight landing, so we could get off the ship and go shopping.

It wasn't long until I discovered that the most exciting place aboard ship by far was the pilothouse. It was like the forward end's family room. During the river passages, the captain and a mate and the wheelsman were always up there, and on the half hour, after checking the spar and the running lights, the watchman came by with his standard report, "Lights are bright." Watches were four hours long. Some men had been together for many seasons and had known each other on different ships over the years. At that time there were no crew rotations for vacations, so a group of men worked together for an entire sailing season and formed (for better or worse) a work family.

Nighttime was the best time in the pilothouse, when the radar and direction finder were lit, and the two-way radio jabbered with shipping traffic. The men talked about the news, their families, their childhoods, and sports, and everybody smoked, drank coffee, and ate donuts. Sometimes, when it was warm, the doors on either side were latched open, and everyone stopped talking as we sailed in the glow of the moon. All you could hear was the turning of the wheel and the lapping of the water on the bow. One night, Dad bet me I couldn't stay up all night, but I had to try. Right before sunrise, it was deadly quiet. The night loosened around the edges; the blackness thinned but it wasn't quite light. The smell was different, a little like fish, and now you could see that the leftover bacon sandwiches from two a.m. had gotten crusty on the windowsill and the fat had hardened. A wind came up, causing a little bounce to the ship. It started to feel humid, and the horizon line became visible, as straight as if it had been drawn with a ruler. It was morning. I had made it!

A few days later, when I'd read all the books I had brought aboard, all the magazines, and all the funnies in the papers from the Soo, I went up to the pilothouse to visit and picked up the *Merchant Marine Handbook* on the chart desk. Dad looked over at me, smiling, and asked how I liked it. I smiled back and said I liked it just fine. I quickly flipped the page I was on and impressed him when I asked some questions about cargo boom stresses and blank spots on the radar. Later, he told everyone at

The perfect moment—calm seas and the glow of the moon. The old-style telescoping hatches are visible. In bad weather they were covered with canvas tarps to prevent leakage.

As morning broke after a long night in the pilothouse, the horizon line looked as straight as if it had been drawn with a ruler.

dinner what a good little sailor I was and told me that I should get my A.B. (able-bodied seaman's license).

I never told him that the chapter I was reading was the one titled "Men's Health," which included anatomically correct pictures and a fascinating section on rashes.

Winter Life

Summer passed quickly and merged into the cold and severe weather of fall. By the first of November, we started to wait again for the end of the shipping season and for Christmas, which was a homecoming for us as well as a holiday—a celebration of safe reentry to extended family, city life, and "land time." When the sailors came back at season's end, I always got to skip school to meet them.

It was eight o'clock—the time I usually left for school—but today was different. The train was due in half an hour. It took only fifteen minutes to get there, but we didn't want to be late and miss seeing the sailors get off. I asked Mom if they were coming into the "castle station," as I called it. It was so grand to go to Duluth's Union Depot. The round turrets made it look like a French château, which made me feel important. We parked and asked what track the train from Chicago would be coming in on, and then we walked down to the gate to join the little group of sailors' wives and children who were already there, shivering from the cold and the excitement. When we heard the train chug around the bend, all the other school-skipping kids and I started jumping up and down as we watched the engine puff toward us and roll to a stop.

Steam shot out from between the wheels, and then the conductor whistled and put down the step stool, and the men detrained: Mary and Peggy's dad, Ellen and Mick's, and Tom and Marshall's,

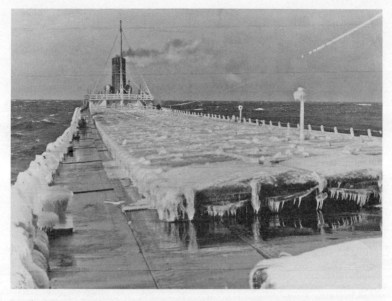

Dad's ship encased in ice on Lake Huron, headed for Ashtabula, in December 1968. Ice, though beautiful, could be dangerous, increasing the weight of the ship by many tons and causing it to ride lower in the water or to list.

and then mine, taller than all the rest and looking like a movie star in his traveling suit, bow tie, and hat. Dad kissed Mom first and then bent down to me so we could rub noses. I was so excited to see him, and, of course, to stop by Bridgeman's to buy the hand-packed vanilla ice cream we needed to make a treat we always had whenever he came home, even if it was in the morning: giant root beer floats.

When we got home, a spruce tree was waiting for us in the yard. While we were gone, my grandfather had delivered it and put it in a snowbank by the back door. He knew that the first thing Dad would want to do was to put up the Christmas tree. He was always in charge of the trimming. He liked to get it "just right."

Usually, Dad was home by the beginning of December, but this year the sailing season had been extra long, and he'd had to

At the end of each season, my father often arrived at the Duluth Depot, which served seven different rail lines. It became a museum in 1973 and now houses several ore malleys, huge retired engines used to pull the ore trains from the mines to the ships in the port.

make a couple of extra trips. It was now only a week before Christmas.

After our root beer float breakfast, Dad unpacked. By lunchtime, his mackinaw was back in the basement closet. His suit and good hat for the train trip were hung up, his bow tie was back in the top dresser drawer, his toothbrush was back in the bathroom holder, and his slippers were back on his side of the bed. Once again, everything was in its place. He was home from another nine months on the water.

The first thing the next morning, we started out with a trip to the hardware store in the big brown Buick Roadmaster. He was happy to drive the car again, and I was happy to be in the passenger seat up front instead of in my usual "safer" place in the back. He had taken the tree into the house to defrost the previous afternoon, and now we were going to trim it. He had saved last year's tinsel, wrapping it carefully around a paper towel roll, but somehow when he took it out, it looked a little frayed, too tangled and not "new," so we were off to see Mr. Neipp, who always put bows on the shovels and an elf on the cash register at Christmas. An hour later, we were back home with four boxes of new tinsel, a new extension cord, a box of replacement bulbs, and a jolly new Santa ornament that I got to pick out.

Dad lit a cigarette, inhaled, and balanced the cigarette on the big brass ashtray on the coffee table. He put on a record—Bing Crosby's *Christmas Carols*—and started to make the magic. First, he made a fresh cut on the trunk, and then he balanced the tree in the stand in front of the window with me holding it while he adjusted the screws. Next came the lights that he fitted over the branches and tightened with little red wooden beads. He moved the bulbs around on the branches, and replaced a few, too, to insure that two orange or red bulbs wouldn't end up too close together. And finally, his specialty—the shimmering silver strands of icicles. Slowly, he unwound the tinsel from the cardboard. One by one, he gently placed each piece, working from front to back, making the branches look like fringed arms. Next came the ornaments. After they were all on, he took the star out of its own special box, with its own white light. He put it on the top, and the tree was done. We turned off the lamps in the living room. The star made a shadow on the wall. The colored lights reflected in the windows. We put the empty boxes temporarily in the corner, and then, Dad said, it was time for a nap.

The house smelled of spruce. He turned over the record, now being the perfect time for "I'm Dreaming of a White Christmas." Then, he lay down on the couch and fell into a deep, snoring sleep. His one arm grew limp and flopped down toward the floor.

He had been gone since March, sleeping when he could, sometimes in the day, sometimes in the night, his days and nights dictated by weather, or narrow waters, landing at the Soo, or "doing" the rivers leading up to the steel mills in Chicago, Toledo, or Buffalo. But now, the tree was up once again, and it was Christmas. He was home with us and safe. I drew close and watched him as he slept. I bent down and looked closely at his arm. The snake's eyes were opposite mine. I had never been this close to it before; usually, his tattoo was covered. The inky blue, dark green, and charcoal grey drawing on his arm depicted a dagger in a sheath with a snake wrapped all around it. The snake had a raised hooded head, yellow eyes, and a forked tongue. Dad's vein pulsed through it. Bump, bump. The snake and I stared at each other. What was he doing on my dad?

I traced it with my eyes for maybe a half hour, over and over again. When Dad awoke, he yawned and smiled and drew in his arms and rolled down and buttoned his sleeves. Then he got up and stretched.

I was just getting up the courage to ask him about his tattoo when Mom came in to look at the tree, and then it was time for dinner, and for some reason, I never did. Later, when I asked my mother about it, she just said, "Oh, you know, he was young and full of vinegar. He got it with the boys on the ship. I think they all got them when they first shipped out."

But there seemed to be something more mysterious about it. It made me wonder about all the places he had been before I knew him.

In January, Mom and Dad went to the Hotel Duluth for the shipmasters' ball. When the big night arrived, I watched my mother spread her hand on the phone table upstairs and paint her fingernails with bright red nail polish. She let the white parts show, placing the polish carefully around the "half moons," and then she walked around the upstairs waving her hands in the air, talking to Dad as he took his dark dress suit out of the closet, brushing it off one more time. He put on his belt, sliding the buckle over to the side as he always did, and then took his best tie from the tie rack where he kept it, already knotted and ready to slip over his head.

Mother put on her nylons, first rolling them up carefully so she could put her foot in them, unrolling them gently so they wouldn't snag, then stretching and pulling them up to hook onto her garters. One year her dress was sleeveless, even though it was winter, and she wore long white gloves.

When her dress was on, she fluffed her hair, put on her dangly earrings, sprayed Tabu cologne behind her ears, and put on her fancy high-heeled shoes, which showed her toes. After one last look in the full-length mirror, she picked up her evening bag and floated down the stairs like a queen. Every year Dad came down and took a picture of her in front of the fireplace. They sat down together for a little while, had a drink and a toast, and then they put on their coats. Mom wore her beautiful mink, which she carefully took out of the zippered storage bag in the closet under the stairs. She handed it to Dad, who held it up for her, showing the silky beige satin lining. Closing her eyes dreamily as she slipped her arms into it, she then gave my grandparents and me careful kisses that left red lipstick smudges on our cheeks.

Dad put on his topcoat and then his hat, cocking it slightly to one side, and they swept out the door and drove off in the big Buick Roadmaster to celebrate the end of another season by dancing above the frozen lake, together.

In the summer, Mom occasionally had the sailors' wives over for lunch, but in the winter when the men were home, she and Dad had their sailing friends over for dinner. Dad built a fire and served highballs in glasses that we used only for special company. They were stored in the cupboard above the refrigerator, and every time he took them down, Mom told me they were a wedding present. There were eight glasses—two pale pink, two blue, two yellow, and two cream-colored, all with gold flowers on them.

I helped put out nuts and cheese and crackers, and when our

Mom poses in our living room for an annual picture before leaving for the shipmasters' ball.

My parents, pictured on the far left of the front row, in the Hotel Duluth ballroom

guests arrived, I carried their coats upstairs to lay them on Mom and Dad's bed. While they ate and talked, I sat at the top of the stairs and listened. Over the background music of Guy Lombardo on the stereo, I heard the wives talking about their auxiliary meetings and discussing their trips aboard ship this year, what the weather had been like, what ports they had gone to, whether they had landed in the daytime or at night, and if they had been able to get off to go "uptown" to shop or do errands. All the wives hated to go to Buffalo, because it was a mile-long walk through the ore piles to the gatehouse, where they could finally call for a taxi.

Mother loved to tell her favorite sailing story. It was about the time she started out for the bathroom when the ship was rolling one way, and how she had just made it to the bathroom door when it started to roll back the other way, which sent her flying across the floor until she hit the bathtub with her knees, causing her to lose her balance and, "head over teakettle," fall into the tub. One time she told about going to pay a visit to Mr. Nageman, the tailor in Ashtabula who had pressed a hole into Dad's suit pants.

All the women talked about meeting ships. They talked about driving in fog and sleet and in the middle of the night, to docks not only in Duluth and Superior, but in Ashland, Wisconsin, and after the advent of taconite, to the new dock at Taconite Harbor, ninety miles up the shore from Duluth. Before the freeway was built and a tunnel drilled through Silver Cliff above the town of Two Harbors, it was often a dreaded ride. The road went around the outside of the cliff, perilously close to the edge, which hung right over the lake hundreds of feet below. Sometimes, if there was fog, they had to pull off before going around the treacherous curve and wait for the fog to lift. Mother told about the time she chanced it, even though there was a blind corner and she could not see the centerline.

The men talked about the amounts of their bonuses, the

bad storms, the dry docks where they had tied up, whom they hoped to get back for crew the next year, who was going to teach radar or navigation school or go to Florida for a few weeks to get away from the snow. Captain Coughlin told long stories and jokes.

"We were comin' into the Straits of Mackinac, you see, and there were sailboats everywhere and a stiff current, you see, and anaways, we were drawin' so deep that we were pullin' 'em in, so I got out the bullhorn and went out on deck and started yellin' and wavin' them away, and anaways, they finally got the message."

Captain Coughlin did most of the talking, but every once in a while Captain Van Orman would say, "I'll be a son of a sea cook!"

I loved hearing the winter voices in the house.

Spring Again

Too soon, the days started to get longer, the orders arrived, and it was spring again. Preparations for departure began, and we went back on "sailing time."

On the first Sunday in March, we drove from Duluth to Superior to attend the Mariners' Service at Pilgrim Lutheran Church. The church extended an open invitation to all the sailors in the Twin Ports to receive a blessing as they prepared to leave for another season on the lakes. My dad was always keen to be early, even though there was a reserved section. We all went, my Duluth grandparents (my mom's parents), my Superior grandparents (my dad's parents, who were always out on the front steps waiting for us to pick them up), my aunt and uncle, and my cousin Barbara, who lived just down the block.

We all squeezed into one pew. The pastor began the service by reading the "Sailor's Psalm": "Some went down to the sea in ships, doing business on the mighty waters; they saw the deeds of the Lord, his wondrous works in the deep." Then we sang the hymn "Jesus, Savior, Pilot Me over Life's Tempestuous Sea," after which my Grandma Michler passed along Kleenex and breath mints. Dad wore his best suit and a navy blue tie with little gold anchors on it. I could feel that people were looking at him and thinking he was handsome.

After the service, we gathered in the basement for a reception,

My grandparents stand on the front steps of their home in Superior, Wisconsin, anticipating with a tinge of sadness but glowing pride the annual church service blessing their son and local sailors as they prepared to sail off to sea in early March.

where the ushers served coffee and lemonade and cookies and cake. Grandma Michler always had her hair done with the bumps still showing from the rollers in the back. She wore her fanciest dress, her white gloves, and her new spring hat. She held Dad's arm tightly as she steered him all around, introducing him to everyone and reminding the minister and those friends of hers who happened to belong to this congregation that this was Willis Carl, that he sailed for The Interlake Steamship Company, that he was now a captain, and that he was her son. To my father and his family, to be recognized in this community was the crowning achievement. My grandfather just stood in the background and smiled.

In June, we could start using our allotted "sailing days." At first, I looked forward to it. The older I got, however, the less excited I was about going aboard ship and spending days away from my friends. When I was old enough to go alone, my mother always insisted it would be good for me to go with Dad right after the school year ended. I knew it was coming. "Why don't you go aboard ship with your dad this trip? It would be nice for

At the reception following the Mariners' Service at Pilgrim Lutheran Church in March 1957, my mother reaches for a plate, with me right behind her and Dad, far left. PILGRIM LUTHERAN CHURCH, SUPERIOR, WI

you to spend some time together," Mom said. "He's due in tomorrow about nine."

I dreaded this. Dad had already told me that he was looking forward to me joining him as soon as school got out. I hated it, because I didn't want to disappoint him, but I didn't want to go. I had just seen the boy I'd liked all year ride by our house twice on his bike, and I had planned to sit on the front steps all week.

Reluctantly, I started to pack: books, cribbage board, cards, notepaper, wool sweaters, jeans, a heavy Lake Superior "summer" jacket, and pictures and addresses of my friends. With a sense of duty, I went.

We sailed out under the Aerial Bridge with happy fanfare. The tourists waved and ran alongside the ship until the end of the pier. Dad blew a salute, and we both waved back at them out the pilothouse window. This was the best part, when you felt like a celebrity, or at least a curiosity. Along the North Shore on London Road the big mansions and gardens looked grand as we sailed by, and the South Shore appeared as a thin line on the right. Then it all melted away as we headed out into the open water of Lake Superior, clear and calm today, but I knew you couldn't trust it.

My father's ship, the SS *Herbert C. Jackson,* passes under the Aerial Bridge in Duluth, Minnesota. DIANE HILDEN

Now Dad could leave the pilothouse. We went below to his quarters. When I looked out the porthole, all I could see was water and sky. I couldn't really tell which was which. Dad recorded the times of loading and leaving in the log, and then leaned back in his swivel desk chair to read the *Duluth News Tribune* and catch up on the hometown news. I started paging through my *Seventeen* magazine. The hot-water heaters ticked and banged, the inside getting hotter as the outside grew colder. There were hooks on everything. Porthole covers were fastened to the overhead, and the desk, chairs, couch, and end tables were fastened to the wall, and all the jiggling hooks croaked softly as the ship began to sway back and forth in the rising wind.

I asked Dad if he wanted to play cards, but I could tell by his eyes that he was slowly slipping into a nap. On arrival, after he had taken the ship through the pier and then the harbor and then maneuvered to the dock, he had come home and mowed the lawn, taken care of some business with Mother, run downtown to pick up some khaki pants and have his glasses adjusted, and now he had taken the ship back out through the close waters. I could see that he was tired. He asked if it was okay to go into his room and lie down for a bit.

I played solitaire and cheated so I could win. After a few games, I took the inside stairway up into the pilothouse where the two-way radio chattered constantly with other ships, giving their locations and weather updates. When the ships were within range, the officers in charge said things like, "Where you bound? Over." Or, "I hear you tied up behind the Sherwin at the Soo," or, "How'd you ride out the wind off the Keweenaw Peninsula?" And then they might sneak in a little personal chatter: "How's the wife and kids?"

Everyone in the pilothouse smoked. If Duluth was their home port, they talked about the families and yards and dogs they had just seen for a couple of hours. I looked at the chart on the desk and traced the shipping lanes to find the one we were in.

Our orders were for Chicago, the Calumet River. I was hoping for Toledo or Cleveland so we could go through the St. Clair River and pretty Lake St. Clair, but not this trip. The Calumet River is tough, very narrow and crowded, with lots of turns and bridges, which meant Dad would be on his feet for long hours. The muscles in his cheeks would be tight, especially if he tried to save money and do it without a tug. Our arrival time was calculated as six p.m., better than one a.m., but not the best. And who knew if we would be delayed by weather somewhere?

Dad would be tired after doing the river, but he would take me ashore. We would probably borrow the dock boss's car and drive around a bit, or maybe take the elevated railway downtown and get back to the ship late, which was always scary, as the fiery steel mills looked and sounded like hell at night, and the path to the ship wound through dark piles of ore and screaming equipment.

Twenty-six hours after leaving Duluth, we would be locking down at the Soo, where the vendors would follow the ship

Dad searches the clouds for clues about the coming weather.

through the lock, selling newspapers, magazines, gum, candy bars, razors, soap, and other items. Everyone aboard ship always bought something, especially cigarettes. The transactions started on the level, but as the ship locked down, the money and items had to be thrown up and down, a skill perfected by both crew and vendors over many years.

In the background, I heard the second cook's dinner bell as he walked around the after-cabin and then up forward. I went in and woke Dad up. He sat on the edge of the bed for a few minutes to get his bearings. After smoothing his thinning silver hair, he put on his captain's hat, then his navy blue jacket with the four gold stripes on the cuffs. I felt proud of him as we walked back. I felt proud to be the ship captain's daughter! He took his place at

Mr. Gregory, left, was Dad's favorite cook. When I was very sick as a child, he sent me a cross with a little glass bubble in the middle through which I could read the Lord's Prayer.

the head of the table in front of the buffet with the mirror reflecting the plates of cherry cobbler, which were already set out. I sat in the first mate's place to his right. The mates had all moved down one place to make room for me, and the wheelsman who would normally sit at the end of the captain's side of the table went to eat in the mess hall for the next five days of the trip.

The second cook, who was also the "waiter," asked my dad how he would like his liver. It was their standard joke. My dad said what he always said: "Over the side." Everyone laughed on cue. Dinner that night was roast beef served on an oval platter with carrots and peas in individual little round dishes all bearing the company flag and the initials PM for the Pickands Mather Company. In another little round dish there was an ice cream scoop–sized ball of mashed potatoes.

The chief, Mr. Tucker, was seated to Dad's left. He talked about his daughters, who were a year older and a year younger than I

The company's "china" featured a red, white, and blue flag with the initials PM in the middle, standing for the company's founders, Colonel James Pickands and Samuel Mather. Even when the company merged with another to become The Interlake Steamship Company, the fleet continued to be known to its employees as the PM Line.

was. Everyone talked a little about the load and about someone's finger that had gotten cut on a wire cable. After dinner we walked forward to Dad's quarters, laughing as we watched the seagulls trying to catch a ride on the mast. We climbed up to the second deck, making the steel rungs ring under our feet. When we turned on the TV, it was all snowy and buzzing, so we played a game of cribbage, and then it was time for bed. "It's sure nice having you here, Dolly," Dad said, and then he went into his room on the starboard side, and I went into the guest quarters on the port side.

The fog began to roll in, and soon the throaty ship whistle started sounding our position every two minutes. Several other ships in the distance began to do the same. Over the whistles, I could hear Dad's contented snoring. I lay in bed watching my sweatshirt on the wall hook sway back and forth to the rhythm of the rocking of the ship. Two and a half days down, and two and a half days up. I wondered what my friends were doing. I wondered if they thought about me. I wondered if somebody had ridden his bike by my house. I fell asleep, dreaming of sailing in the South Seas with a handsome lover.

When we started to see the North Shore again on our return trip, I put my hot rollers in, getting ready to disembark in Duluth. Dad was getting ready, too, to enter the port.

"Want to come up to the pilothouse with me?" he asked, sticking his head in the bedroom door. "But you'll have to take out those whatchamacallits!"

He stood there chuckling. I could tell he really wanted me to come up with him. After all, I thought, we would have only a few more hours together, so I took them all out. I put the bobby pins back in the jar, stuck my hair in a ponytail, and went up.

It was still open water. Dad didn't have to be "in the window" quite yet, so he told the second mate to stay there, and he went back to the big desk and got the chart out of the drawer. He showed me Two Harbors off to our right. We had passed the Apostle Islands several hours before, but he pointed them out on the chart, knowing that I had been there. He told me about the time he had taken coal to Washburn and then sailed out to Duluth between Bayfield and Basswood and Oak Islands, and how tricky it was because of the currents and shoals.

Then he closed the drawer, walked up to the window to relieve the mate, looked back at me, and said, "I think you should give the wheelsman a break and take a try at the wheel. I was thinking you should do some wheeling this trip, and here we are already at the end of it."

I thought he was kidding, but the wheelsman smiled and said, "Here you go, matey." He stepped off the little platform, looked at me, and said, "Steering steady as she goes."

Dad said, "Go ahead." When the wheelsman went over to

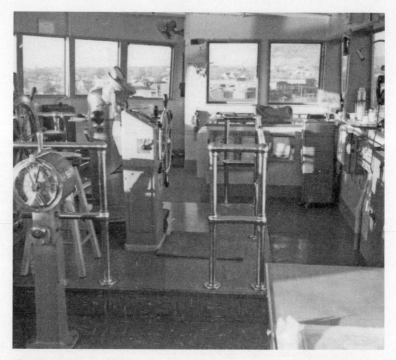

The wheel in the pilothouse stood on a platform, elevating the wheelsman so he could see out of the surrounding windows.

the thermos and started to pour some coffee, I could see that this was serious. I stepped up on the platform, and Dad said, "Now put your hands on ten and two of an imaginary clock and take hold of the spokes of the wheel in those places." The big wooden wheel was still warm from the wheelsman's hands, smooth and smelling like furniture polish.

"The trick to wheeling is that you have to anticipate the rate at which the ship responds," Dad said. "You have to get a sense of how long you have to keep the wheel over before it catches. If you hold it over too long one way or the other, the ship turns back and forth too much. Then you're always overcorrecting it, and it will zigzag. Every ship handles differently, so a good wheelsman learns how long it takes for the rudder to respond

Mother takes the wheel with her hair up in pin curls under her bandanna, which would come off for dinner at the captain's table. The humidity, she lamented, often caused her hair to go flat.

on the particular ship he's wheeling. In open water, what you're aiming for is to keep a straight wake.

"Now look down in front of you and you'll see the compass. When you turn the wheel and the ship moves, it will look like the compass is moving the opposite way of the ship. That's because the ship moves around the compass. You have to get used to that. When I say, 'Steady as she goes,' you want to keep the lubbers line on the compass from moving either way."

"Do you ever take the wheel?" I asked. "Like if the wheelsman isn't doing it right?"

"Nope, I don't. By the time you're wheeling a ship like this, you know what you're doing. My job is to analyze and chart the course. The wheelsman's job is to get the ship to do it. Your mother's done it! So let's practice."

He continued, "Take a half-turn to starboard and wait and see how long before the ship grabs hold so you can get an idea of what it feels like."

I turned the wheel several spokes to the right and nothing happened, so I turned it some more.

"Remember," Dad said, "it takes a while for the ship to answer you. The wheel shaft is about a block long, so just be patient. Another thing, when I give an order, you repeat it. That's an international sailing law to make sure that the captain knows that the wheelsman has heard exactly what the captain wants."

"Aye, aye, sir!" I said.

Then he repeated, "Take it one-half turn to the right," and I said, "One-half turn to the right," and in about a minute, it started to turn, a lot. I panicked and quickly turned the wheel the opposite direction to get it to come back. A long minute later, it started to go left, but then it went a little too far. It felt scary, and I wondered out loud what the men on deck were thinking with the ship, all of a sudden, waltzing back and forth.

The wheelsman laughed. I turned the wheel back the other way.

"Check your wake," Dad said. I looked back, and it looked like a Z. "Now you can see how that works. You have to make smaller adjustments. Just let the wheel go now and get itself back to midships and then keep her steady as she goes."

"Back to midships," I said, and I let the wheel go. It went back by itself to the middle, again.

"Remember, just small adjustments are enough to keep her going straight. Think of yourself as helping the ship find its path. You really have to feel her, how she likes to move. Every ship is different. See that ship in the distance? Keep the steering pole right on it."

"Aye, aye, captain," I said. "Steering pole on the ship."

"Attagirl," he said.

I kept a pretty straight wake until a little land breeze came up. Then it began to get wavy, and we started to slip off course as the wheel got harder and harder to hold onto. Dad didn't say

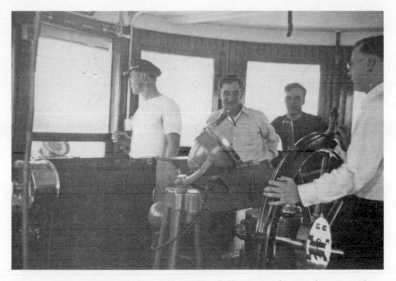

In the pilothouse, Dad, left, is pictured with the mate, the watchman, and the wheelsman, who had just come on duty for his four-hour shift.

anything, but the real wheelsman could see I was struggling. After a few minutes, he got up and stood a few steps behind me.

He kept hovering there, and then he finally said, "What do you think, Cap?"

Dad said, "It's okay, Charlie, let her keep trying. You have to learn how to handle a little chop." I stuck it out for a while longer, and then the wind got stronger, and the waves started to pound harder. The Aerial Bridge at Duluth was starting to come into view, and there were several ships at anchor, and one coming toward us.

The wheelsman cleared his throat, and then he said again, "What do you think, Cap?"

Finally, Dad said, "Okay, Charlie, keep her on the bridge."

Charlie said, "On the bridge, sir." As he stepped up, I stepped down.

After passing through Duluth's Aerial Bridge, the SS *Herbert C. Jackson*
makes a left turn toward a dock just past the grain elevators across the bay
in Superior, Wisconsin. DIANE HILDEN

I stayed around for a little while. I had a donut and played
with the slide rule on the chart desk, and then I asked if it was
okay if I went back down. Dad didn't answer, as just then the
phone rang and he started talking to the captain of the ship we
had been following. It was just starting to enter the canal. He
told Dad there was a strong current running out of the bay today.
There was a "saltie" just letting go of its lines over at the grain
dock, the man said, and it would probably meet us at the turn
by Rice's Point right after we got through the canal.

Dad thanked him for the heads-up, lit a cigarette, blew for the
bridge, and then he looked down. At the entrance to the canal,
Mom was waving on the walkway in front of the lighthouse. Dad
blew her the captain's salute, one long blast and two short ones,
then grabbed the big bullhorn, shot out the door, and yelled,
"Forty minutes to the dock!" as we passed her.

I ran out too and waved at Mom and all the people gathered

From the pilothouse, Dad calls for a tug, with the radar situated to his left. In tense situations, I could see Dad's cheek muscles contract.

to watch what always felt like a triumphal entry. Dad had already dashed back and started to call for a tug, seeing that there was both current and traffic.

While he was calling, I slipped down the stairs, went into the bedroom, and plugged my rollers back in. As I was waiting for them to warm up, I could hear the ongoing background chatter of the shortwave radio upstairs. Then I heard my dad say, "Did Ann go down already?" I parted my hair to put a roller in my bangs, and when I looked in the mirror to stick the bobby pin in, for the first time I wondered: Did Dad ever secretly wish I were a boy? But I knew he wouldn't trade me.

November Gales

Every year my dad was a captain, I took at least one trip with him, until I was nineteen. That year, I went to school in Paris to study French.

At first, it was exciting to be away, and I didn't even think about home. But by the end of the summer, I was homesick. I even started to miss the rhythmic drone of the foghorn and the cold, damp flannel-and-fleece Lake Superior "summer" days. It was the first time since I was twelve that I hadn't spent time aboard ship with my dad. Now I missed it, and I knew how much he must have missed me.

When a letter came from him, I couldn't wait to open it. I thought I knew what it would say: How long is it until you're coming back? The summer hasn't been the same without you.

What a surprise when I opened it and read: "Hi Honey, hope all is well. I'm having a great year so far. I've never had it so good. I have a crackerjack first mate, darned good second and third mates, the best cook in the fleet for a steward, a 2nd cook whom everyone wants, and the best chief I ever had. On top of that, I have a humdinger of a ship, which is a beautiful handler. It has a splendid master's quarters, and your mom was just aboard for a trip to Chicago where we got to see *Around the World in Eighty Days,* and it's been beautiful weather."

He didn't say anything about me at all! He didn't even write

During a late November day on Lake Superior, the ship rides low in the water from a heavy load and the weight of the ice.

My dear daughter A-N-N:
Know what? I'm very, very lonesome
for you. I haven't seen you and you haven't
seen me for darned near SEVEN months.

In Dad's letter to me in Paris, he calls me "A-N-N," as he sometimes did. I had heard that he wanted to name me something a bit more glamorous, like Gloria, but Ann, which was my mother's middle name, won out.

again for several months. The next time I heard from him was November, the meanest month of the shipping year with its steel grey skies, high winds, and waves that wash over the deck, gluing the hatches and the cables and the railings and the ladders together with ice.

This time, the letter began, "My Dear Daughter A-n-n: Know what? I'm very, very lonesome for you. I haven't seen you and you haven't seen me for darned near SEVEN months. We've been at anchor now for twenty-four hours in Lake Michigan. The wind has raised the water level in the lake six feet. We can't get into port, and I'm sitting here at my desk thinking I can't wait to see you for Christmas. Glad it's about over once again."

It was a long November.

Our Last Trip

After I graduated from college, Dad arranged for me to take one last trip. I packed the usual: rain gear, books, stationery, and cards. We left Duluth at night. The red blinking lights of the TV and radio towers on the hills receded steadily as once more I left the city behind. Our destination was Toledo, Ohio. We were to get there in the daytime, which would allow us to get off and go "uptown."

Dad said he knew where there was a great specialty popcorn store with caramel corn with lots of nuts, and he wanted to find a camera shop to take a look at the new Polaroid cameras. We talked a little more about what we might do: find a nice place for lunch, maybe even go to a movie. Then we looked out the front porthole at the deep darkness and went to bed. I pulled back the floral bedspread in the fancy passenger quarters, crawled under the quilt, and was just falling asleep when I could feel the ship start tossing up and down restlessly. I heard the plastic glass in the bathroom fall off the sink, roll across the floor, and hit the wall. The wind had shifted. Holding onto the end of the bed, then reaching for the chair to keep my balance, I opened the screen door and stole out to the bow to feel the cooling air. I looked down—so far down. The waves curled against us as we divided them with our bow, now lifting us up a few feet, then dropping us back down again before continuing their ride along the hull.

Dad waters his beloved pink-and-white petunias in our favorite spot on the "veranda."

When they hit the back cabin, the lights on the stack blurred in the spray. Up, down, clouds hiding the moon, no lights of any ships around us, no sound except for the rhythmic boom and swish of the water. I was sailing again.

By morning the wind had died down and it was clear and sunny. Dad worked on payroll and I sat out on the deck and read. He joined me for a while, watered his flower boxes, and then called for the porter to bring up lunch. Before dinner that night, we walked around the after-cabin a few times for a little exercise, and then we went into the dining room for something I ate only aboard ship—corned beef and cabbage.

Sailing on the SS *Herbert C. Jackson* through the St. Mary's River just below the Soo Locks

When the moon came up, we began to see the outlines in the distance of several ships starting to get in line to go through the river leading up to the Soo Locks. Standing out on the bow, Dad made me look for the North Star just to make sure I remembered how to find "true north." Since ancient times, he said, Polaris has been the "sailor's star." We now have modern navigational devices such as the gyrocompass, but those depend on human power sources that can fail. The North Star never goes out, he laughed. It's still a sailor's best friend.

He pointed out Cassiopeia, important because it's one of the constellations visible year-round in the northern sky. We stood there silently in a bowl of stars. The ship rocked gently in the night wind. "It's so awesome out here," I said. "It feels like we're floating through time and space."

"We are, Dolly," he said, still gazing upward. "We are."

We went up to the pilothouse together. When we nudged up to the breakwater, the deckhand called out the familiar "up against." When we entered the lock, I held my breath as Dad expertly guided the ship to a gentle stop inches from the end of the lock. As we sailed down the St. Mary's River, we began reminiscing. We remembered the time I had made a bed in the equipment room off the observation lounge (living room), just for fun, and how I liked to help the men sweep the deck. The best was when it was so hot one trip that Dad rigged up a fire hose to spray me on the life raft.

The bells in the buoys chimed as we sailed past them. The houses ashore looked cozy with distant yard lights. After several hours, we reached the open water of Lake Huron and went to bed. From Dad's bedroom I could hear Debussy's "Clair de Lune" playing softly on his tape player. We both slept soundly until noon.

When we got to Toledo the following day, it was eight a.m., a lucky landing time for going ashore, though Dad had been up since four a.m. to take the ship in to the dock. Dad said that the guard here always let him borrow his car, so we were set for "going up the street," as the sailors say. I was really looking forward to it.

When the unloading was under way (unloading took a lot longer than loading—it was done with buckets called Huletts), we climbed down the ladder. Then we picked our way along the dock under the gyrating iron arms that were busily grabbing bites of iron ore from the hold and dumping them onto the towering stockpiles.

The dock boss was in the guardhouse. He and Dad clapped each other on the back and shook hands. The guard said he was happy to lend us his car. Dad thanked him and then inquired about his wife, Gladys, who was ill. Then the yard manager came in. Dad had known him for thirty years. He was credited with having put window boxes filled with petunias and geraniums on the retired locomotive that stood out by the maintenance shed

To unload "down below," a man went down into the hold, grabbing and lifting out cargo by operating the controls from a little compartment that he sat in just above the bucket.

on a section of old track. Dad introduced me all around, and then, through the open door, we saw a man in a sport coat and tie approaching. He strode in and shook hands with Dad. They went outside and talked for a long time. Then they came back in. I thought Dad was finally ready to go, but instead of taking the car keys off the guard's desk, he just looked at me. I looked back at him expectantly. I didn't get it. I was anxious to get started on our time together.

"This is my daughter, Ann," Dad said. "Ann, this is the fleet manager. He's here from the home office. He drove over from

Cleveland to take a look at the leaky seam that I reported last week. I thought we were going to check it out when we got back up above, that they were sending someone from Fraser Shipyard in Superior to inspect it then, but he said he decided to drive over and take a look at the situation firsthand when he heard we were coming to Toledo. We'll have to go back aboard. Maybe we can get going in an hour or so."

I glared at the man. We went back aboard. Dad sprayed DDT on his office screen door, which was already covered with black flies, and then the two men sat in front of the fan on Dad's desk and talked about rivets and reviewed the problem. The leaky seam was in the first hatch. After a while, they went out on deck. I went into the guest room, where I was staying, closed the port-holes and the door to keep out the noise, and started writing a letter. "Dear Mom, 'Hello' from Toledo, from the dock, that is. We were just about to leave the guardhouse to go uptown when a man from home office arrived. You know what that means!"

Two hours later, I heard Dad come back in. When I walked into the observation room, he looked at me and put his finger up to his lips. He stood still and listened for a minute, and then he turned up the volume on the weather channel, which was always on low in the background. He didn't like what he heard. He went back out on deck to look at the sky.

"Barometric pressure falling," he said when he came back in, and he sat down and began mapping out a cell that was coming up the Ohio River Valley, commenting that it would probably hit us sometime before midnight. After a few minutes, his head slipped down on his chest. His cheeks relaxed, his hand loosened, and he dozed off, dropping the pencil onto the floor. I walked over and turned down the mechanical weather voice. Bad weather meant he would probably have to stay up most of the night.

I looked at him. He was still tall, thin, and handsome, but

Aboard the SS *Herbert C. Jackson,* Dad and the fleet manager look down into the first hatch. The deck above them shows the windows of the lounge, available to us when the ship was not carrying passengers.

wrinkles were beginning to form around his eyes and mouth. In his short-sleeved shirt, I could see that his tattoo was fading. The yellow in the snake's eyes had almost disappeared. I thought back to the night when Dad had become a captain, how excited he was. I wondered if he still felt that way. How many hundreds of nights had he stayed up? How many rivers had he navigated in fog? How many tense landings had he made? How many wild storms had he sailed through? How many family events had he missed? How many fleet managers had he dealt with? The older I got, the harder this life seemed. I wondered if the older man would choose the young man's dream again.

He woke up with a start and looked out the porthole at the thermometer, noting the ninety-degree temperature. Then he checked the humidity—ninety percent. It clearly was going to be a "blister." I could tell that his energy had dipped. It was too much to get off the ship again. I made a decision. "We don't have to go uptown, Dad. That caramel corn would just get stuck in our teeth anyway."

He laughed and accused me of wanting to avoid going down the ladder again. I pretended that I was feeling tired and had gotten out of the notion.

It was the right call. He didn't argue. He swiveled around in his chair and reached up to his shelf of tapes and chose one to put on his new reel-to-reel tape recorder—Rachmaninoff's Concerto no. 1, recorded by Van Cliburn. He said it reminded him of the sound of the wind, and the rhythm of the waves crashing on the deck. I wondered if it also reminded him of another vision he'd once had of himself. I knew that as a young boy he had taken piano lessons seriously and with promise. I had heard that at one time he wanted to be a pianist. What had happened to that dream? He still loved classical music, and all his ships had loudspeakers on the deck through which Bach and Beethoven occasionally wafted over the water. In the winter, he still

> * * *
>
> The Schwab is probably the only 680-foot, floating "symphony" on the Great Lakes. Mrs. Michler, with a quiet smile, says that the Schwab's crew often pulls in cables to Bach, Beethoven and Brahms. The captain said that when the Schwab goes through the Soo Locks he turns up the sound and then he and the crew watch the amazed faces of the many tourists who crowd along the walkways and viewing platforms next to the locks. The captain has a wide selection of the world's most beautiful music.

An article in the *Superior Telegraph* details the music periodically piped through loudspeakers on my father's ship. While he never became a professional pianist as he had planned when he was a young boy, Dad retained a lifelong love of classical music, its grandeur and harmonies seemingly audible to him in the winds and waves of the lake.

practiced his recital pieces, especially the octaves in the Turkish March, over and over again.

He looked at me, smiled, and pulled out the middle desk drawer, taking out the wooden board with the ivory pegs. We started to play cribbage, a game that he loved. He was suspicious that I was still secretly counting on my fingers, and I accused him of pegging an extra hole now and then, although I knew he wouldn't. He won every game, except one.

When we were finished, I looked at him, and all of a sudden it just came out. "How did you get into this life, Dad, when you were so young?"

"Hmm. That's quite a question," he said. He hesitated for a moment, and then he told me that actually it was pretty simple. A summer sailing job became his career, and his career became his life. "You can't always tell which way your life is going to go," he reflected. He told me that a well-known and well-respected Great Lakes captain, Captain T. A. McDougall, lived right behind his house in Superior and that my grandfather knew him. His dad asked Captain McDougall if he could give my dad a job aboard his ship the summer he was sixteen.

Dad, second from left, with other crew members aboard ship in Buffalo in 1930, in his early days of shipping

I told him that I couldn't believe that my grandfather would do that, or that my grandmother would allow it. He reminded me that his father had been a railroad conductor, that he grew up when young men still served as apprentices, and that he'd started working on the railroad himself when he was sixteen.

"Times were different then, you know. In fact, my dad was already talking to me about being a plumber, but I didn't want anything to do with that. My mother wanted me to be a music teacher. She had already talked to my piano instructor about working for him and continuing my lessons that summer I first shipped out. I loved the piano, but I was sixteen, and I was up for an adventure. I wanted to go. Growing up in a busy port, the call of the water was pretty powerful to a young man."

He talked about hearing ships' whistles, and train cars coupling at night. And when the wind was blowing, he could see and feel the dust of the largest ore docks in the world. The waterfront was bustling. It was exciting. He remembered watching the big boats maneuvering in the busy harbor, gliding under the bridges. In the winter they were laid up in the shipyard, towering over a part of the town. Sometimes he and a friend hiked over just to look at them. They looked important and grand. One summer day they even went over to Duluth, he said, and spent the whole day sitting on the break wall, watching the ships sailing in under the Aerial Bridge and out again over the horizon line.

It was a different world, he said, sailing across vast Lake Superior, learning how to use winches and sounding boards, being part of a crew, landing in different ports and going uptown on adventures with the seasoned sailors. "It was an eye-opener. I had never been out of the Twin Ports before. That's when I stopped using the name Willis and started calling myself Bill," he chuckled.

He said he loved the fresh smell of the water, the spectacular sunrises and sunsets, and sailing through the stars at night. Everything was big—the ship, the noise, the docks, the cargo, even the meals. Landing and casting off, departures and arrivals, there was just something about it, he said. He started as a porter, but he was continually after the mate to get him up to the forward end. By midsummer he finally made it, as a deckhand. "I was all over that ship," he said.

When he went home to go back to high school in the fall, he felt like kind of a hero to the other kids. Laughing out loud, Dad said, "Especially to Captain McDougall's daughter, I hoped! I was hooked. After that summer, I thought, boy, this is it. Someday I'm going to be up in that pilothouse and sail under the Aerial Bridge as the master of my own ship. Someday, my dad will be proud, and even my mother. Someday I'm going to be like Captain McDougall and have four stripes on my sleeve and be The Old Man."

I wondered how he had met my mother, if he was away all the time. After he graduated from high school, he said, he did sail full-time. During lay up in the winter, he went to Superior

My dad as a young deckhand

State Teachers College to give school a try and to make his mother happy. He always ended up shipping out again in the spring, however. He met my mother at school one winter. She was studying to be a teacher, he said, and came over the bridge from Duluth every day. It took a while, he grinned, but eventually he convinced her to take a chance on getting connected with a sailor.

I could just hear her saying, "I fell in love with a sailor, not sailing!"

He lifted his arm to smooth down his hair. "What about the snake and the dagger, Dad? I always wanted to ask you about it. It used to scare me when I was little," I confessed. "When and where did you get it? It never seemed like something you would have."

He looked at me and then looked out of the porthole, smiled, and said, "Those are the kinds of stories that start, 'Once upon a time a long, long time ago.' All that was a long time ago, Dolly."

I wanted to ask him more about that time, but I could see that his mood was shifting. He didn't say any more, and I didn't ask any more questions.

At six p.m. we went back for dinner—cold cuts tonight. At seven-thirty we climbed up to the pilothouse together. He checked the weather again. He rang up the chief to give him the latest update, and then he called the mate and told him to get

Mom and Dad, then a second mate, aboard the SS *James Pickands*

out the tarps and have the crew start battening down the hatches. As I watched the men unrolling and clamping down the heavy black canvas tarps to ward off leakage in case of a heavy sea, I saw a jagged burst of lightning out of the corner of my eye. It cut a yellow line through the black sky in the west, and then came a crack of thunder. The wires on the mast started to bang together in the rising wind. I shivered, wondering how severe the weather was going to be.

"Are you ever afraid, Dad?" I asked.

It didn't seem like he heard me. His eyebrows narrowed as he walked over to the chart desk. He pulled out the drawer and drew out the chart of Lake Erie. Putting it on top of the desk, he got out the big magnifying glass, the quadrant, and the slide rule. He lit a pipe, squinting out the window at the sky and then down at the radar. He was working now, but a few minutes later I heard him mutter, "When you're in the midst of it, you're too busy to be afraid. Can't think about being afraid until it's over."

At eight p.m. we threw off our lines and started on our way

The ship in a rather common state of "rolling"

back up to the Soo, hoping to get ahead of the storm. For a few moments, behind us, a sunbeam broke through the gathering clouds and shone golden on downtown Toledo.

About eleven p.m., we got some heavy wind and rolled steadily for about an hour, but the brunt of the storm veered north and missed us.

"Pretty lucky this time," Dad told everyone at breakfast.

We finished our last trip together in fair weather.

Batchawana Bay

Eventually, I married, moved away, and had a family. At the age of sixty-three, unable to climb the ladder anymore, my father retired. He and my mother moved to Tucson, Arizona, for a new kind of life. I was relieved to have them safely there, away from the sailing life. But that life *was* their life, and though far from water, my father, "The Old Man," once more drifted out to sea.

We were visiting for Easter. We had just finished our dinner and were getting up to go into the kitchen to dye Easter eggs. Everything was already set up on the kitchen table—a dozen boiled eggs, cups of different-colored dyes, and little decals of chickens and bunnies and ducks. Dad, however, stayed seated and surprised us by launching into a story. He began talking as if he were addressing an unseen audience.

"It was just after Easter that year, our first trip upbound in the spring, and we got into a blinding snowstorm above the Soo. There was a sixty-mile-per-hour wind and twenty-foot seas, and we were getting blown farther and farther off course."

Mother looked at me. I looked at my husband, and the three of us sat back down.

The children exchanged glances, silently agreeing that this story might take a long time. On tiptoes, they kept heading into the kitchen and started writing their names on their eggs with the white crayons.

Pointing to an imaginary chart on the tablecloth, Dad said, "I got out the charts and the big magnifying glass, and I started to look for islands or inlets, reading the small numbers on the chart to check the depth. The closest bay, Batchawana Bay, was not an official shipping area, no lines designating shipping lanes anywhere near. But it was our only chance for the lee."

In Tucson, Dad is caught in a spontaneous reflection on his sailing life.

Beads of sweat began to form on his forehead.

"The waves were beating up the ship pretty badly," he went on, "and the hatches were starting to take on water. I looked again at the chart and made my decision. It's our only hope, I decided. We've got to try for the bay. I knew that when we turned to go in, the wind would hit us broadside. We'd either ride it out, or we wouldn't. I got on the intercom and told everyone what we were doing, and told them to hang on tight to something, and we started to make the turn."

Mom began folding her napkin into smaller and smaller squares. Had she heard this story before? I wondered.

"The wind hit us full force on the starboard side," Dad said. "I hung on for dear life to the ship's telegraph as we kept tipping lower and lower until all I could see was water out of the port side window of the pilothouse," Dad went on. "We stopped and hovered for a second or two, and then a rogue wave bounced off the

This storm in Batchawana Bay was a classic Lake Superior storm, the likes of which made a lasting imprint on my father's sailing life. The SS *Edmund Fitzgerald* went down with all hands only fifteen miles away from this location in 1975.

rocks and tossed us back the other way, rolling us back over on our starboard side. Under my feet it suddenly felt light, and I said to myself, this is it, we're going over, and we just stayed there, pitched over on our side for what seemed like a long, long time."

The ship's clock in the living room chimed the half hour.

"Suddenly, there was a momentary decrease in the wind," he went on, "and the ship started to come back, slowly righting itself. A second later, another wave hit us across the stern, and we rode it into the bay. I rang up the chief, who reversed the engines, and the ship finally floated to a stop. We dropped the anchors, and we sat there in a snowstorm all night."

Just then, the children in the kitchen plopped their eggs into the purple and green cups. One of the eggs inadvertently hit the orange cup, which tipped over, and the orange dye started dripping onto the floor, making a mess. Mom dropped her napkin and jumped up, exclaiming, "Oh, glory, the children!" She dashed into the kitchen, grabbing dishcloths and paper towels, and began cleaning up.

Oblivious to the commotion, Dad continued. "When daylight came and the snow and wind had stopped, I saw that the bay was half a width smaller than it had appeared on the chart, and the ship almost filled it up. I looked at how we had come in through the rocks in the dark. We had made it, but the crew was not impressed.

"When we finally got out of there and made it to Duluth, everyone except the officers quit and got off," he said. "All those boys went back to the mines on the Range or the farms along the South Shore where they'd been recruited. One severe storm was enough for them. Their sailing days were over."

In the kitchen, the mess got mopped up. The purple and green eggs came out with the children's names written clearly, and they were delighted.

Dad looked out the glass door at the desert and said, "That was the one time in all my years on Lake Superior that I thought I was going to die."

I looked up and saw Mom standing in the doorway. She and Dad locked eyes.

"Were you married then?" I asked. "Oh, yes," Mom said, still looking at Dad. "That was the first spring that he shipped out as a captain. When he got back to Duluth, he insisted we go right downtown, and he bought me my beautiful mink coat."

The coat in the zipper bag!

I turned to Dad, and now I asked him, "Would you choose the sailing life again, Dad, if you could do it over?"

He looked with pride at the handsome wooden model of his last ship mounted on brass brackets on the wall. Then he turned to Mom, and to me. Looking down at the pale wrinkled snake on his arm, he smiled wistfully, but he didn't say anything. He knew that we knew the answer.

Dad's Last Command

It was in the spring, just after the ice broke up, that my dad died. After his funeral in Duluth, my mother, my husband, the children, and I decided to go down to Canal Park. Just as we were unbuckling our seat belts, we heard the loudspeaker from the Marine Museum Visitor Center announce that the 694-foot-long SS *Herbert C. Jackson* was departing the harbor bound for Chicago with twenty-two thousand tons of taconite pellets. This had been Dad's last command! I shouted to everyone to run for the pier.

We dodged through the parking lot as fast as we could, but by the time we pushed through the crowd around the popcorn wagon, with a half block still to go, the ship had already gone under the Aerial Bridge, and its after-cabin, with its big black stack and orange band, was gliding by.

We tried to catch up to it, to run alongside it, but it kept slipping farther ahead of us. Finally, we had to give up. Panting, we stopped and watched it clear the lighthouse at the end of the breakwater, and then we saw the flag on the stern begin to flap in the off-shore breeze.

The others got cold and began to walk back. But Mom and I stayed.

I envisioned a handsome young captain stepping away from the pilothouse window, saying, "I'm going downstairs now, boys," then, "Keep her steady as she goes, Charlie," and "It's all yours

The SS *Herbert C. Jackson,* Dad's last command, leaves the Twin Ports of Duluth-Superior for yet another trip "down below." DIANE HILDEN

now," to the mate. Soon the ship looked like a little toy, then like a brown dot, then just a smudge on the horizon.

"Goodbye, Willie," I heard Mother whisper. We stood there watching until the ship melted into a cloud, and then it was gone, due at the Soo in twenty-six hours, and thirty-six hours later at a steel mill in Chicago, where another ship captain's wife and daughter would be waiting for it, down below.

The experience of command of a ship at sea is unforgettable; it is without parallel or equal. The responsibility is heavy, but the rewards—which become embedded in the very fabric of your life—are priceless.

FROM COMMAND AT SEA

Acknowledgments

My thanks to Kate Thompson, senior editor at the Wisconsin Historical Society Press, for her vision of memoir as history and her interest in mine.

Thanks also to developmental editors Sara Phillips for drawing out my father's Wisconsin heritage and Erika Wittekind for honing the work and teasing out additional dimensions, as well as Elizabeth Boone for seeing it through production.

John Toren was coauthor in many instances. His sensitivity, language skill, and mechanical expertise helped nudge the story to what it wanted to be, and his idea of bringing it to the Wisconsin Historical Society is the reason the book in this form exists.

The list of further acknowledgments is daunting.

I thank my parents, who saved pictures and articles and who wrote journals with a sense that this life mattered. Childhood friends Ann Jenkins and Jeffrey Long shared my experience of growing up in a maritime community on a lake with an alluring and relentless horizon and thought I should share this regional life. My husband, Herb, and children, Amy and Lee, contributed through suggestions from their own memories. Louis Jenkins read, commented, and encouraged, as did Marit Nowlin, Peggy Dollinger, Professor Catherine Guisan, Bill and Linda Lundberg, Laura and Peter Merriam, Jan and Bill Munson, Linda Smith, Anita Zager, Fred and Jan Martin, Mara Hart, and Judith Josephson.

Local people connected to the shipping industry were essential in providing the correct facts and vocabulary. Davis Helberg, former director of the Seaway Port Authority, graciously arranged for me to attend a Propeller Club meeting, where I met mariner icons Dick Bibby, Wes Harkins, and Captain Gil Porter, who knew my father. Captain Porter volunteered his ongoing help and sat with me in his kitchen going through the manuscript word by word to make sure it was "right." Great Lakes pilot Shawn Mckenzie also met with me early on, made suggestions, and connected me with Ellen Leu, whose father was the storyteller in "Winter Life" and with whom I had a delightful exchange regarding our experiences as ship captain's daughters. Brian Thierry told me about loading. Mary George from the Lake Superior Maritime Visitor Center was an ongoing source of valuable information. She told me about the weight of ice on ships and also sent me to *Lake Superior Magazine* editor Konnie LeMay, who looked at the collection of material and asked the critical question, "What's the story?"

Archivist Laura Jacobs from the Jim Dan Hill Library at the University of Wisconsin–Superior supplied important data and found the picture of my father's first command.

Editors went through it in evolving stages: Julie Jensen, Gail Trowbridge, Jill Breckenridge, Evelyn Klein, and Connie Wanek, all with critical input, and professors Calvin Roetzel, Paula Cooey, and Jean Jacobson were cheerleaders.

Jeff Shroeder got me untangled from many computer panics, and Amy Jenkins was the very first person who combined the initial vignettes and laid them out in a way that suggested they might become a book.

J'ai Lisa's interest at Kinko's was heartening.

Finally, my sincere thanks to those I may have forgotten but whose ideas, information, and affirmation have made an invaluable contribution to the final product.

MARY T. GEORGE

About the Author

Ann Michler Lewis grew up in Duluth, Minnesota, where she lived from 1944 to 1967. She graduated from the University of Minnesota, Duluth, and taught English at Duluth East High School. Since 1972 she has lived in St. Paul, Minnesota, where she and her husband raised their son and daughter, making periodic family pilgrimages back "home" to Lake Superior. She has privately published a book of poems and sailing stories called *My Duluth,* now out of print. Fascinated by how the power of place shapes the human story, she thinks British writer Lawrence Durrell has captured it best: "We are the children of our landscape. It influences behavior and even thought, in the measure to which we are responsive to it."